Date: 8/3/12

SPACE ● SCIENCE

Meteors

Simon Rose

MEDIA ENHANCED BOOKS
AV2 BY WEIGL™
ADDED VALUE ● AUDIO VISUAL

www.av2books.com

Go to **www.av2books.com**, and enter this book's unique code.

BOOK CODE

R92994

AV² by Weigl brings you media enhanced books that support active learning.

AV² provides enriched content that supplements and complements this book. Weigl's AV² books strive to create inspired learning and engage young minds in a total learning experience.

Your AV² Media Enhanced books come alive with...

Audio
Listen to sections of the book read aloud.

Video
Watch informative video clips.

Embedded Weblinks
Gain additional information for research.

Try This!
Complete activities and hands-on experiments.

Key Words
Study vocabulary, and complete a matching word activity.

Quizzes
Test your knowledge.

Slide Show
View images and captions, and prepare a presentation.

... and much, much more!

Published by AV² by Weigl
350 5th Avenue, 59th Floor
New York, NY 10118

Website: www.av2books.com   www.weigl.com

Library of Congress Cataloging-in-Publication Data

Rose, Simon, 1961-
Meteors / Simon Rose.
    p. cm. -- (Space science)
Includes index.
ISBN 978-1-61690-634-4 (hardcover : alk. paper) -- ISBN 978-1-61690-638-2 (softcover : alk. paper)
1. Meteors--Juvenile literature. I. Title.
QB741.5.R667 2012
523.5'1--dc22
                          2010050413

Printed in North Mankato, in the United States of America
1 2 3 4 5 6 7 8 9 0 15 14 13 12 11

062011
WEP290411

Weigl would like to acknowledge Getty Images and NASA as its primary photo suppliers for this title.

Every reasonable effort has been made to trace ownership and to obtain permission to reprint copyright material. The publishers would be pleased to have any errors or omissions brought to their attention so that they may be corrected in subsequent printings.

SENIOR EDITOR: Heather Kissock
ART DIRECTOR: Terry Paulhus

Meteors

CONTENTS

Rocks
from Space

A meteor is a streak of light in the sky. It is caused by a piece of rock from space that falls into Earth's **atmosphere**. The rock's speed may be thousands of miles (kilometers) per hour. Moving through the air at high speed, the rock becomes very hot. That is why it shows up in the sky as a streak, or trail, of light. Meteor streaks are sometimes referred to as **shooting stars** or **falling stars**. Meteors usually glow for about a second. Only rarely will a meteor trail last for a few minutes.

Space rocks are called **meteoroids**. Most of them never come near Earth. Meteoroids may be as tiny as a grain of sand or as large as a huge boulder. A few may even be the size of a house or bigger. The majority of meteoroids that enter Earth's atmosphere are small. Most of these rocks get so hot as they travel through the air that they burn up completely before they reach the ground.

Extremely bright meteors are sometimes referred to as **fireballs**. They are also known as **bolides**. Some scientists use the name *bolide* only for a fireball that explodes or produces a noise that may sound like thunder.

Space rocks occur in many different shapes as well as many different sizes.

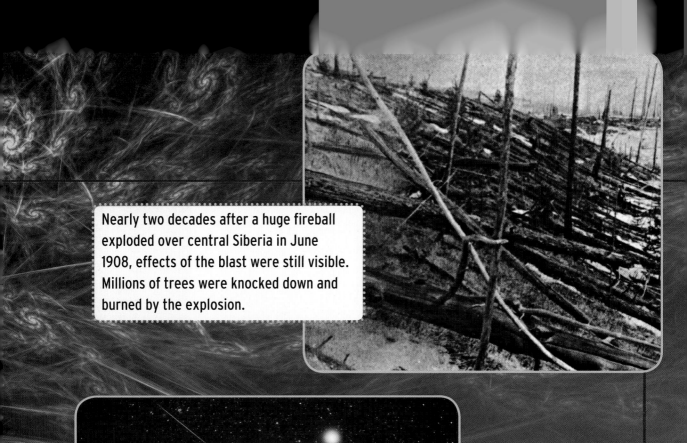

Nearly two decades after a huge fireball exploded over central Siberia in June 1908, effects of the blast were still visible. Millions of trees were knocked down and burned by the explosion.

Meteors are usually seen on dark nights.

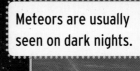

BRAIN BOOSTER

Meteors generally look white, but a fast-moving fireball may appear blue or green. This is because of a reaction between the air and the object's motion.

Sometimes, the color of slower-moving fireballs depends on what the rock is made of. Meteoroids made primarily of iron may appear to be yellow.

Showers and Storms

Meteors are usually not bright enough to be seen in daylight. On almost any night, though, a few meteors can be seen, as long as the sky is dark enough for good visibility. At certain times during the year, meteor showers occur. In a meteor shower, hundreds or even thousands of streaks of light can be seen in a single night. An especially intense shower is known as a meteor storm.

Meteor showers can occur in all parts of the world, including remote mountain locations where they may be seen by very few people.

The meteors in a shower usually originate, or "radiate," from one place in the night sky. This area is called the radiant. The shower gets its name from the **constellation**, or group of stars, in which the radiant lies. One of the most active showers that occurs regularly every year has its radiant in the constellation Perseus. At its peak, in August, the number of meteors in this shower can exceed 60 per hour.

The meteor shower that originates in the constellation Perseus is called the Perseids.

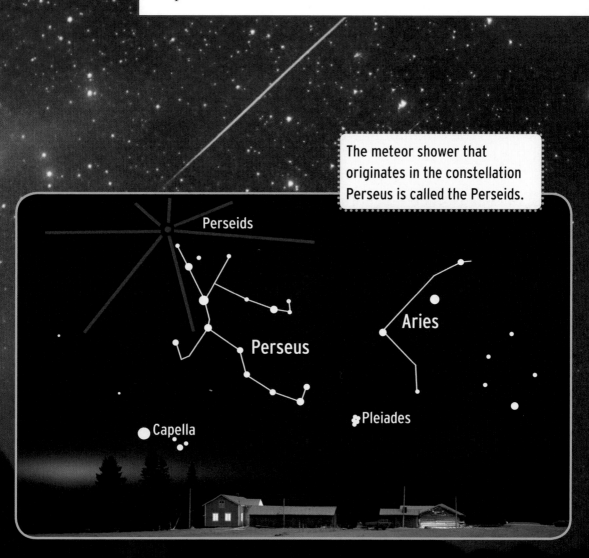

Perseids

Perseus

Aries

Pleiades

Capella

Meteors
through History

For thousands of years, most people thought that meteors were just something that happened in the atmosphere, like lightning. Some people imagined that the streaks of light came from the clouds, like rain, snow, or hail. This way of thinking about meteors is why they have the name they do. The word *meteor* comes from a Greek word meaning "high in the air." The same Greek word is the origin of *meteorology*, the name for the scientific study of weather.

Around the late eighteenth century and early nineteenth century, a few scientists proposed that certain rocks found on Earth actually came from space. This idea slowly gained acceptance as scientists began to pay more attention to meteors. American **astronomer** Denison Olmsted and French scientist Jean-Baptiste Biot were two researchers who made important discoveries.

Denison Olmsted was a professor at Yale University at the time he studied meteor showers.

In April 1803, rocks rained from the sky at the French town of L'Aigle. Biot studied the rocks that reached the ground and found that they could not have originated on Earth. In November 1833, the Leonid shower, or Leonids, filled the sky with thousands of meteors. Olmsted studied the meteors' paths and concluded that they must have come from a cloud of particles in space.

Some scientists continued to believe that meteors originated in the atmosphere. However, as astronomers continued to study objects in space, more and more evidence built up that meteors came from beyond Earth's atmosphere.

The Leonid meteor shower of November 1833 was visible throughout the eastern United States.

Comets and Asteroids

Meteoroids are just one example of the countless objects in the **solar system** that are smaller than planets. Other kinds of objects include comets and **asteroids**, both of which are larger than meteoroids. Scientists now know that comets play a role in causing **meteor showers**. Occasionally, asteroids may also.

Comets are composed of gas, ice, and dust along with rock. Some have **orbits** that take them near the Sun. When a comet comes close to the Sun, its temperature increases. Some of its icy material vaporizes, or turns into gas. As a result, the comet develops a tail, which may be millions of miles (kilometers) long. Also, bits of rock get left behind in the comet's path. This debris gradually spreads out along the comet's orbit. If Earth passes through the comet's orbit, some of the debris may enter the atmosphere at high speed and burn up, producing a meteor shower.

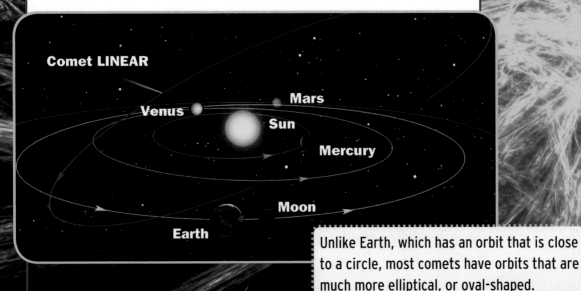

Comet LINEAR

Venus · Mars · Sun · Mercury · Moon · Earth

Unlike Earth, which has an orbit that is close to a circle, most comets have orbits that are much more elliptical, or oval-shaped.

The Leonid shower, for example, is caused by Comet Tempel-Tuttle. This comet takes about 33 years to complete its orbit around the Sun. In some places along its path, there is a huge amount of debris from the comet. In years when Earth passes through such a spot, the Leonids can create an intense meteor storm. Halley's Comet, which sweeps by Earth approximately every 75 years, is responsible for two annual showers. One is the Orionids, a shower that peaks in late October. The other is the Eta Aquarids in early May.

Unlike comets, asteroids are made up mainly of rock. One of the most active annual meteor showers, the Geminids, seems to be caused by an asteroid called 3200 Phaethon. Scientists are not sure how a solid object such as an asteroid could have a trail of debris that can cause a meteor shower.

Halley's Comet has been observed for centuries, going back to at least 240 BC.

THINK ABOUT IT
One explanation proposed for the Geminids is that 3200 Phaethon is really a dead **comet**. In other words, it long ago lost its gas and ice. Its rocky part continues to orbit the Sun, as does the stream of meteoroids the supposed comet once produced. Can you think of another possible reason why an asteroid could be linked with a stream of meteoroids?

Falls and Finds

Every year, millions of meteoroids fall into Earth's atmosphere. Most are simply bits of dust. Only some of the pieces of material entering the atmosphere are large enough to produce a visible meteor. Just some of the rocks producing meteor trails actually make it to the ground. Large meteoroids are more likely than small ones to make it all the way through the atmosphere. Some large meteoroids, because of their makeup, explode before reaching the ground. There also are meteoroids that vaporize when they hit the ground, leaving little trace of themselves. A meteoroid that lands on the surface without being destroyed is called a **meteorite**.

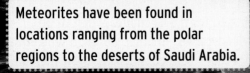

Meteorites have been found in locations ranging from the polar regions to the deserts of Saudi Arabia.

Meteorites are either "falls" or "finds." Falls are meteorites that are recovered right after they are seen falling through the atmosphere or hitting the ground. Many meteorites are not discovered by people until long after they have landed. These are referred to as finds. There are about 1,000 falls now in museums around the world. The number of meteorite finds is around 40,000.

Most meteorites are thought to be fragments of asteroids or comets. A few discovered in Antarctica, Libya, and elsewhere are different. Their makeup suggests that they came from Mars or the Moon. Scientists think these rocks may have been blasted into space when a large object, such as an asteroid, hit Mars or the Moon.

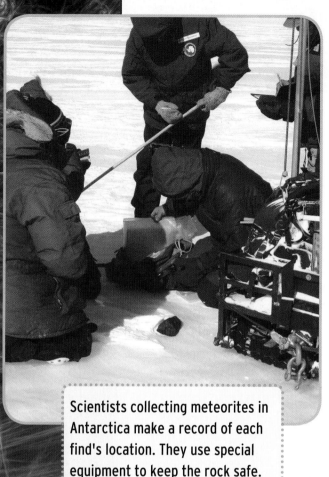

Scientists collecting meteorites in Antarctica make a record of each find's location. They use special equipment to keep the rock safe.

BRAIN BOOSTER

Each year, an estimated 30,000 to 80,000 meteorites larger than 0.7 ounce (20 grams) in size fall on Earth. Most of them are unlikely to be seen or found, since they fall in the ocean or in areas where no one lives.

No one is known to have been killed by a meteorite, although there are a few reports of persons being hit by one. In August 1992, a 13-year-old boy in Mbale, Uganda, was struck in the head by a meteorite weighing about 0.1 ounce (3 grams). The object's fall was slowed by tree leaves, and the boy was not seriously hurt.

The Makeup of Meteorites

Meteoroids from comets are often not solid enough to survive passing through the atmosphere. For this reason, most meteorites found on Earth are thought to be asteroid fragments. They are divided into three main types. These are called stony, iron, and stony-iron.

Stony meteorites contain minerals rich in silicon and oxygen, with smaller amounts of iron, magnesium, and other **elements**. Most belong to the group of meteorites known as chondrites, which account for around 86 percent of all meteorites. Chondrites contain small round glassy particles called chondrules. Stony meteorites without chondrules are called achondrites. They account for about 8 percent of meteorites.

About 5 percent of meteorites are iron meteorites. In addition to iron, they generally contain a fair amount of nickel. These rocks are thought to come from the metal core of an asteroid. Stony-iron meteorites account for only about one percent of meteorites. They contain silicon-based stone and iron-nickel metal in about equal amounts.

Scientists believe that the meteorites called chondrites are more than 4 billion years old.

The stony-iron meteorites called pallasites contain colorful bits of glass-like material. Often considered beautiful, pallasites have even been used in jewelry.

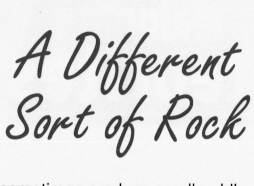

A Different Sort of Rock

Meteorites sometimes produce small, oddly shaped glassy rocks called tektites. Typically black or olive-green in color, tektites are usually no larger than 5 inches (12 centimeters) in size. They are produced when a large object from space hits the ground with a great deal of force. The impact melts some surface rock and may toss drops of the resulting liquid material into the air. The drops cool as they fly, turning into solid tektites. The tektites may land a considerable distance from the impact point.

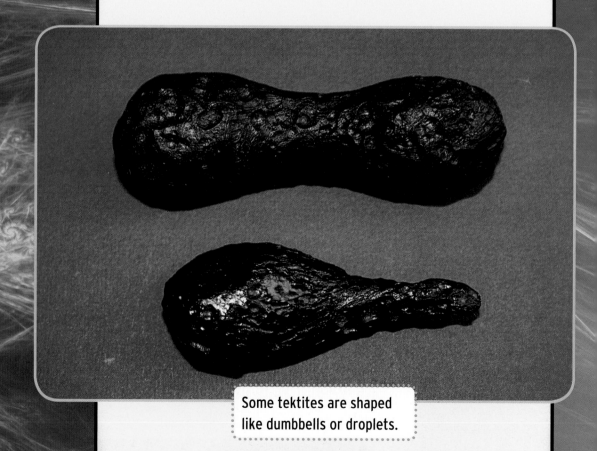

Some tektites are shaped like dumbbells or droplets.

Major
Meteorites

The largest meteorite ever discovered was found in 1920 at Hoba West, a farm in the African country of Namibia. It is an iron meteorite and weighs about 66 tons (60 metric tons). The meteorite has never been moved since its discovery, because it is so enormous.

Several large iron meteorite pieces have been found at Cape York, Greenland. People living in the area used the meteorites for centuries as a source of metal. At the end of the nineteenth century, American explorer Robert Peary took three of the pieces, including the largest one, and sold them to the American Museum of Natural History in New York City. The largest piece, called Ahnighito, or "the Tent," weighs about 34 tons (31 metric tons). Another large piece, weighing about 22 tons (20 metric tons), was found in 1963. Known as Agpalilik, or "the Man," it can be seen at the Geological Museum of the University of Copenhagen in Denmark.

The Hoba meteorite in Namibia is the largest naturally occurring piece of iron on Earth.

The largest meteorite ever found in the United States is also an iron meteorite. It was discovered in the Willamette Valley of Oregon. Weighing about 15 tons (14 metric tons), it ranks as the sixth largest meteorite in the world. Now known as the Willamette meteorite, it is on view at the American Museum of Natural History.

The Willamette meteorite's huge pits were caused by sulfuric acid, formed when sulfur within it combined with water from the environment.

BRAIN BOOSTER

An object as big and heavy as the Willamette meteorite had to cause some damage when it landed. No signs of damage have been found in the Willamette Valley. Some scientists suspect that the object landed elsewhere and was moved to the area by massive floods at the end of the last **Ice Age**.

On October 9, 1992, a bright greenish fireball streaked across the eastern United States. The object exploded into many pieces. One of the pieces, weighing about 27 pounds (12 kilograms), slammed into the trunk of a car parked in a driveway in Peekskill, New York.

Impact Craters

When a large object from space hits the ground with great force, the impact usually forms a crater. A crater is a bowl-shaped or saucer-shaped hollow in the ground. Very large impact craters are sometimes called basins.

More than 175 impact craters have been identified on Earth. The Moon and some other bodies in the solar system each have many more. One reason why Earth has relatively few is that most meteoroids burn up before they can smash into the ground. Small objects that do make it to the surface may be slowed by the air to such an extent that they do not hit the ground hard enough to produce a crater. On the other hand, the air cannot significantly slow down a massive object that enters the atmosphere at a high speed. Such an object will very likely produce a crater if it hits the ground.

Large impact craters can be hundreds of feet (meters) wide.

There is another major reason why relatively few craters are seen on Earth. Many craters formed by impacts in the past have disappeared. The rims of craters may be eroded, or worn away, by wind or moving water. In addition, Earth's layer of surface rock is affected by forces from below, which sometimes cause land to sink beneath the ocean.

The largest known impact crater on Earth is the Vredefort Dome, southwest of Johannesburg, South Africa. About 2 billion years ago, the area was hit by a huge object that made a crater roughly 185 miles (300 kilometers) wide. Rock below the surface was pushed down by the impact and then rebounded to produce a raised rock "dome." Most of this dome eroded away over millions of years.

A ring of hills about 43 miles (70 kilometers) wide is about all that can be seen of the Vredefort Dome today.

BRAIN BOOSTER

Meteorite craters have been found on every continent except Antarctica. They may well exist in Antarctica, too, but the ice covering the continent makes it difficult to definitely prove their presence.

The object that produced the Vredefort Dome may have been as much as 6 miles (10 kilometers) wide. The object hit with enough force to vaporize an estimated 17 cubic miles (70 cubic kilometers) of rock.

Major North American Craters

The best-preserved large impact crater on Earth is in northern Arizona, about 35 miles (56 kilometers) east of Flagstaff. Known both as Meteor Crater and as Barringer Meteorite Crater, it is about 0.75 mile (1.2 kilometers) wide and 560 feet (170 meters) deep. It was formed about 50,000 years ago by an iron meteorite that was about 160 feet (50 meters) wide. The object probably disintegrated when it hit the surface.

The Chicxulub Crater measures about 110 miles (180 kilometers) across, but it cannot be seen. It was formed 65 million years ago and today lies beneath Mexico's Yucatán Peninsula and the Gulf of Mexico. The impact that caused it may have resulted in the disappearance of half of all the species, or types, of plants and animals then in existence. The species that died out included most types of dinosaurs.

Sensors that pick up differences in rock and other materials can detect remnants of the Chicxulub Crater below Earth's surface.

Scientists believe that the object that created the Chicxulub Crater must have been huge. It may have been 6 to 9 miles (10 to 15 kilometers) across. It smashed into Earth with an estimated force 2 million times greater than the largest nuclear bomb ever tested. This colossal impact likely caused wildfires, earthquakes, and volcanic eruptions. Huge clouds of ash probably covered the planet for several years, blocking sunlight and causing a drastic drop in temperature.

The object that caused the Chicxulub Crater led to a series of environmental problems. Those dinosaurs that survived the initial impact are believed to have died as a result of the aftermath.

GET CONNECTED

For a map showing the location of the Chicxulub Crater and a number of other notable impact craters, go to http://geology. com/meteor-impact-craters.shtml.

Craters
on Other Worlds

Impact craters are found on many bodies in the solar system. They cover the planet Mercury, most asteroids, and the majority of moons circling planets. Earth's Moon is covered with craters. Unlike Earth, it has virtually no atmosphere to protect it from impacts, and there is no wind or rainfall to erode the craters.

Like Earth, the planets Mars and Venus have relatively few craters. Impact craters on these planets tend to become buried or eroded over time. The planets Jupiter, Saturn, Uranus, and Neptune do not have craters. They are mainly made of gas. They do not even have a surface like Earth's on which craters can be formed.

There are some enormous craters in the solar system that are known or believed to be the result of meteoroid impacts. Many scientists think, for instance, that an impact basin may cover most of the northern **hemisphere** of Mars. Sometimes called the Borealis Basin, it is about 5,300 miles (8,500 kilometers) wide and 6,600 miles (10,600 kilometers) long. The floor of the basin is 2.5 to 5 miles (4 to 8 kilometers) lower than the planet's southern hemisphere.

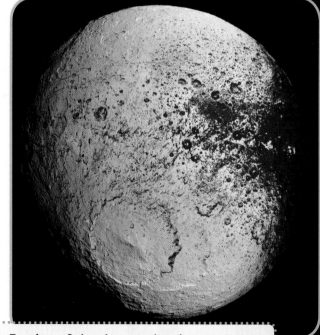

The crater Turgis on Saturn's moon Iapetus measures 360 miles (580 kilometers) across. That distance is about two-fifths of the moon's entire width.

Mars has some smaller, but still huge, features in its southern hemisphere that many scientists believe are impact craters. One is the Hellas Basin, which is more than 1,300 miles (2,100 kilometers) wide. Another is the Argyre Basin, measuring roughly 1,100 miles (1,800 kilometers) across.

The Moon also has a super-sized impact crater, near its south pole. This basin is known as South Pole–Aitken. It is about 1,600 miles (2,600 kilometers) wide.

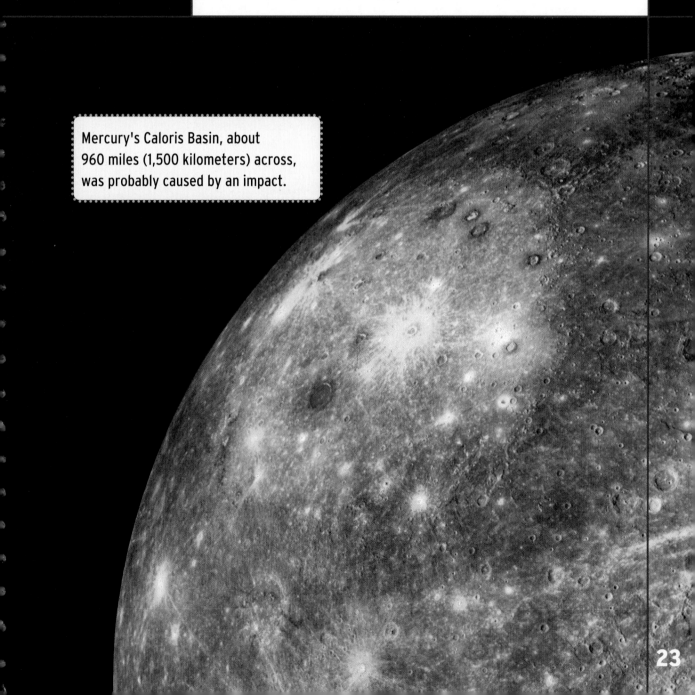

Mercury's Caloris Basin, about 960 miles (1,500 kilometers) across, was probably caused by an impact.

Working with
Meteors

Several types of careers are available for people interested in studying meteors, meteorites, or meteoroids. These jobs require a strong background in science and, usually, one or more advanced university degrees. In addition to getting an advanced degree, people often begin their careers with a couple of years of postgraduate training.

ASTRONOMER
Astronomy is the study of the universe. Astronomers tend to specialize in a particular aspect of the field, such as planets, smaller bodies in the solar system, the Sun, stars, the search for extraterrestrial life, or the origin of the universe. Many astronomers are professors at colleges or universities and do research as well as teach. Others work at observatories or museums.

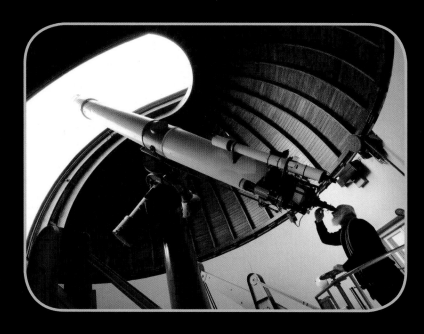

ASTROPHYSICIST

Astrophysicists are astronomers who focus on questions involving the principles of physics. Physics is the scientific study of **matter**, energy, forces, and the motion of objects. Some astrophysicists concentrate on the physics of a certain part of the universe, such as bodies in the solar system. Most astrophysicists teach astronomy, physics, or mathematics at a college or university while also doing research.

GEOLOGIST

Geology is the science concerned with rocks, minerals, and the history of Earth's development over billions of years. Geologists who specialize in the rocks known as meteorites are sometimes referred to as meteoricists or meteoriticists. In addition to geology, they need to be familiar with astronomy, astrophysics, chemistry, and metallurgy, or the science of metals. These scientists try to understand the makeup of meteorites by identifying the minerals in them. Many meteoroids were formed at an early stage in the solar system's development. Studying meteorites found on Earth can help scientists learn about the solar system's formation.

Looking for Shooting Stars

On almost any night, it is possible to see a shooting star, as long as the sky is dark enough. The night sky in many areas gets a great deal of light from streets, vehicles, and buildings. In these places, it may be almost impossible to see any meteors. Moonlight can also interfere with the ability to see meteors. If the sky is dark but no meteor shower is occurring, it may be necessary to wait a while for a shooting star to appear.

When there is a meteor shower, sky watchers should face toward its radiant in order to see as many meteors as possible. For the Leonid shower, for example, the radiant is in the constellation Leo. People hoping to see Leonid meteors should look for that constellation.

Open land with a clear view of the sky improves the chances of sighting a meteor.

Meteor watchers who stay inside will likely miss all but the brightest fireballs, which are rare.

Meteor watchers do not need to use binoculars or a telescope. A meteor is usually easy to see with normal eyesight. Also, binoculars or a telescope make it hard to view large areas of the sky at one time. Looking at a broad area of the sky is the best way to see as many meteors as possible.

Several well-known meteor showers appear every year. They include the following.

SHOWER	CONSTELLATION OF RADIANT	APPROXIMATE DATE OF PEAK
Lyrids	Lyra	April 21–22
Eta Aquarids	Aquarius	May 5–7
Delta Aquarids	Aquarius	July 28–30
Perseids	Perseus	August 12–13
Orionids	Orion	October 21–22
Leonids	Leo	November 16–18
Geminids	Gemini	December 13–14

GET CONNECTED

To learn the precise peak dates for key meteor showers in most parts of the United States, sky watchers can go to http://stardate.org/nightsky/meteors.

Test Your
Knowledge

1 Where does the word meteor come from?

A Greek word meaning "high in the air."

2 What is a meteoroid?

A space rock

3 What is the largest meteorite ever found on the surface of Earth?

The Hoba meteorite, found in Namibia

4 Which major meteor shower occurs every November?

The Leonids

5 Meteors that appear yellow are likely to be caused by an object made mostly of what?

Iron

6 Which two major meteor showers are caused by Halley's Comet?

The Orionids and the Eta Aquarids

7 What is a fireball?

An extremely bright meteor

8 What is the name for the area of the sky from which a meteor shower originates?

Radiant

10 Why are relatively few impact craters found on Earth?

Earth's surface is active, and impact craters tend to get worn away or buried over time. Also, meteoroids passing through the atmosphere may slow down or may even explode before reaching the surface.

9 What is the name of the crater caused by the meteorite thought to be responsible for the disappearance of most dinosaurs?

Chicxulub

Glossary

asteroid: a rocky object that has an orbit around the Sun and is bigger than a meteoroid but smaller than a planet

astronomer: a scientist who studies planets, stars, galaxies and other objects in space

atmosphere: the layer of air that covers Earth's surface

bolide: a fireball, especially one that explodes or makes a sound similar to thunder

comet: an object in the solar system that is composed of gas, ice, dust, and rocky debris

constellation: a group of stars that appear to form a shape or pattern in the sky

elements: the basic substances that make up matter

falling star: a meteor

fireball: an extremely bright meteor

hemisphere: half of a planet or other large object in space, such as the northern hemisphere or southern hemisphere of Mars

ice age: a period of time in Earth's history when ice sheets covered much of the planet

matter: a general name for the substance or substances that make up any object

meteorite: a rock that is found on the surface of a planet, asteroid, or moon and has fallen from space

meteoroid: a rock in space; meteoroids may be as tiny as a grain of sand or nearly as big as a small asteroid

meteor shower: the appearance of an unusually large number of meteors in the sky; some showers occur at the same time every year

orbit: the path that one body in space follows as it circles around another, such as Earth's orbit around the Sun and the Moon's orbit around Earth

shooting star: a meteor

solar system: the Sun and all the objects that orbit it

Index

Log on to www.av2books.com

AV² by Weigl brings you media enhanced books that support active learning. Go to www.av2books.com, and enter the special code found on page 2 of this book. You will gain access to enriched and enhanced content that supplements and complements this book. Content includes video, audio, web links, quizzes, a slide show, and activities.

Audio
Listen to sections of the book read aloud.

Video
Watch informative video clips.

Embedded Weblinks
Gain additional information for research.

Try This!
Complete activities and hands-on experiments.

WHAT'S ONLINE?

Try This!	Embedded Weblinks	Video	**EXTRA FEATURES**
Complete engaging activities that further explain meteors.	Learn more about meteors.	Watch a video about meteors.	**Audio** Listen to sections of the book read aloud.
Write a biography about an important person.	Find out more about a notable person.	Check out another video about meteors.	**Key Words** Study vocabulary, and complete a matching word activity.
Test your knowledge of space.	Learn more about pursuing a career studying meteors.		**Slide Show** View images and captions, and prepare a presentation.
Play a fun interactive activity.	Find out more about the technology used to study meteors.		**Quizzes** Test your knowledge.

AV² was built to bridge the gap between print and digital. We encourage you to tell us what you like and what you want to see in the future.
Sign up to be an AV² Ambassador at www.av2books.com/ambassador.